HAL•LEONARD

UKULELE PLAY-ALONG

AUDIO ACCESS INCLUDED

PLAYBACK+
Speed • Pitch • Balance • Loop

Songs *for* Beginners

Play 8 Easy Songs in the Key of C with Professional Audio Tracks

To access audio visit:
www.halleonard.com/mylibrary

2141-1906-8663-1859

Ukulele by Mike Butzen

ISBN 978-1-4803-9386-8

HAL•LEONARD® CORPORATION

7777 W. BLUEMOUND RD. P.O. BOX 13819 MILWAUKEE, WI 53213

Visit Hal Leonard Online at
www.halleonard.com

UKULELE NOTATION LEGEND

THE MUSICAL STAFF shows pitches and rhythms and is divided by bar lines into measures. Pitches are named after the first seven letters of the alphabet.

TABLATURE graphically represents the ukulele fingerboard. Each horizontal line represents a a string, and each number represents a fret.

Notes:

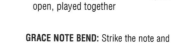
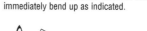

Strings:

2nd string, 3rd fret | 1st & 2nd strings open, played together | open F chord

---

HALF-STEP BEND: Strike the note and bend up 1/2 step.

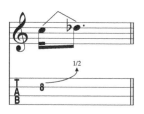

WHOLE-STEP BEND: Strike the note and bend up one step.

GRACE NOTE BEND: Strike the note and immediately bend up as indicated.

SLIGHT (MICROTONE) BEND: Strike the note and bend up 1/4 step.

BEND AND RELEASE: Strike the note and bend up as indicated, then release back to the original note. Only the first note is struck.

PRE-BEND: Bend the note as indicated, then strike it.

VIBRATO: The string is vibrated by rapidly bending and releasing the note with the fretting hand.

HAMMER-ON: Strike the first (lower) note with one finger, then sound the higher note (on the same string) with another finger by fretting it without picking.

PULL-OFF: Place both fingers on the notes to be sounded. Strike the first note and without picking, pull the finger off to sound the second (lower) note.

LEGATO SLIDE: Strike the first note and then slide the same fret-hand finger up or down to the second note. The second note is not struck.

SHIFT SLIDE: Same as legato slide, except the second note is struck.

TRILL: Very rapidly alternate between the notes indicated by continuously hammering on and pulling off.

TREMOLO PICKING: The note is picked as rapidly and continuously as possible.

Additional Musical Definitions

 (accent) • Accentuate note (play it louder)

 (staccato) • Play the note short

D.S. al Coda • Go back to the sign (𝄋), then play until the measure marked "**To Coda**," then skip to the section labelled "**Coda**."

D.C. al Fine • Go back to the beginning of the song and play until the measure marked "**Fine**" (end).

N.C. • No chord.

 • Repeat measures between signs.

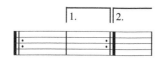 • When a repeated section has different endings, play the first ending only the first time and the second ending only the second time.

NOTE: Tablature numbers in parentheses mean:

1. The note is being sustained over a system (note in standard notation is tied), or

2. The note is sustained, but a new articulation (such as a hammer-on, pull-off, slide or vibrato) begins, or

3. The note is a barely audible "ghost" note (note in standard notation is also in parentheses).

CONTENTS

Eleanor Rigby

Words and Music by John Lennon and Paul McCartney

wear-ing a face ___ that she keeps ___ in a jar ___ by the door, ___

who is it for? ___ All the lone - ly peo -

- ple, where do ___ they all ___ come from? ___

To Coda

All the lone - ly peo - ple, where do ___ they all ___ be - long? ___

1. 2. D.C. al Coda Coda

Additional Lyrics

2. Father McKenzie writing the words of a sermon that no one will hear,
   No one comes near.
   Look at him working, darning his socks in the night when there's nobody there,
   What does he care?

3. Eleanor Rigby died in the church and was buried along with her name,
   Nobody came.
   Father McKenzie wiping the dirt from his hands as he walks from the grave,
   No one was saved.

Have You Ever Seen the Rain?

Words and Music by John Fogerty

Jambalaya
(On the Bayou)

Words and Music by Hank Williams

La Bamba

By Ritchie Valens

D.S. al Coda 1

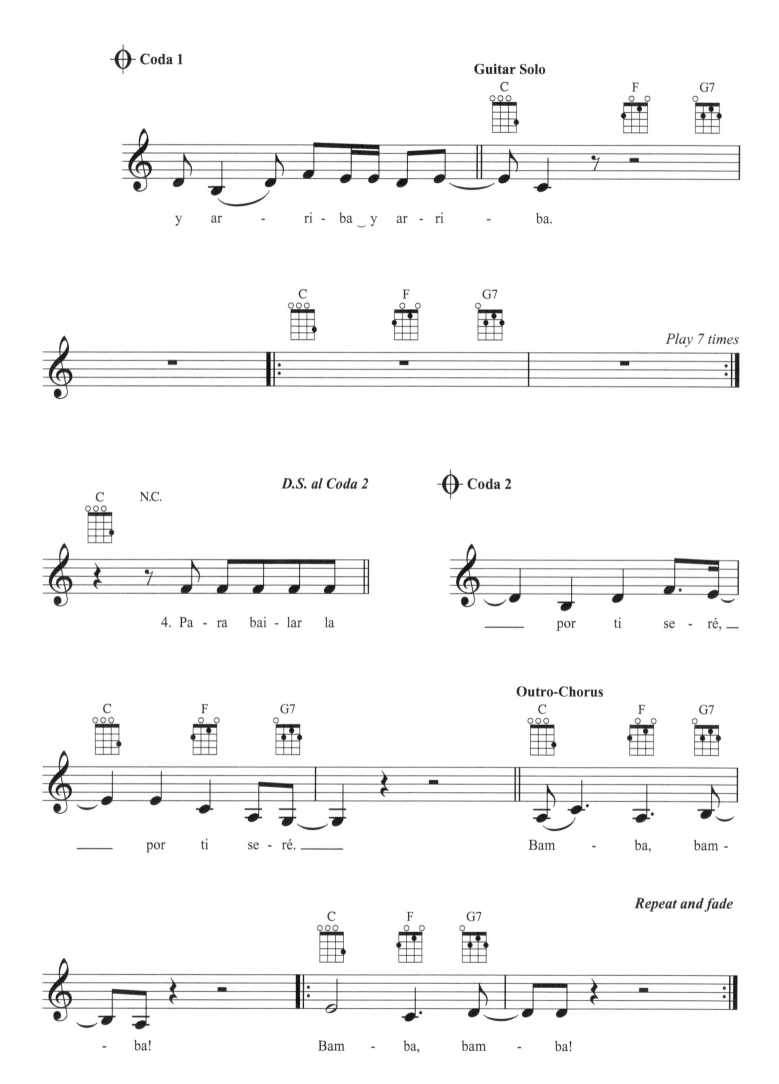

Learning to Fly

Words and Music by Tom Petty and Jeff Lynne

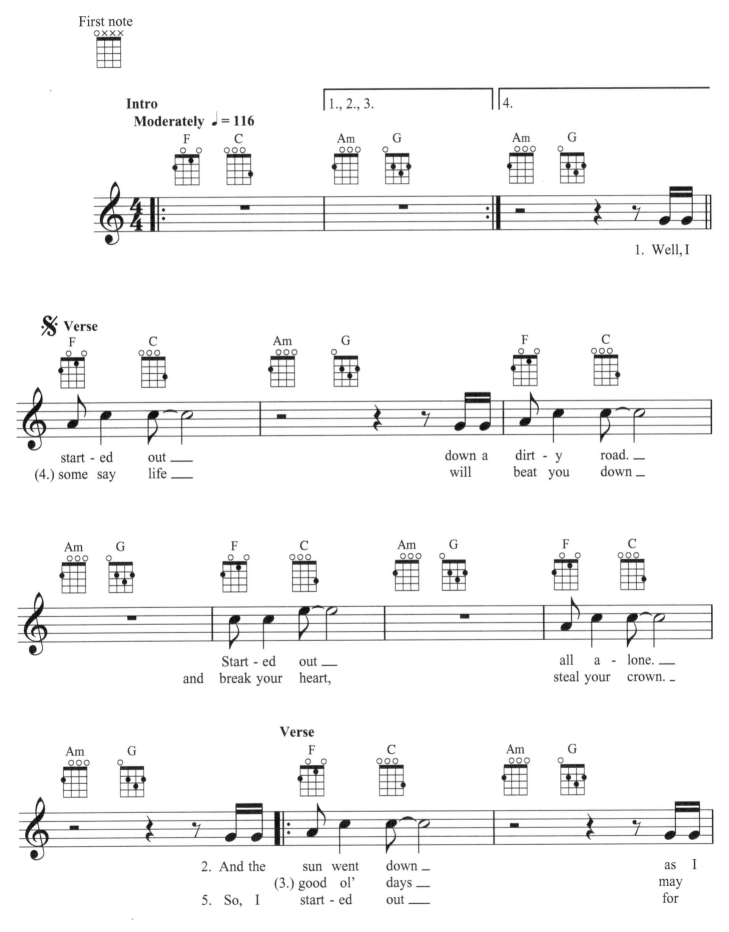

crossed the hill, ____
not re - turn ____
God knows where. _

and the town lit up, ____
and the rocks might melt ____
I guess I'll know _

the world got still. ___
and the sea may burn. __
when I get there. _

I'm
I'm
I'm

Chorus

learn - ing to fly ____
learn - ing to fly ____
learn - ing to fly ____

but I ain't got wings. _
but I ain't got wings. _
a - round the clouds. _

Com - ing down _
Com - ing down _
What goes up ____

is the
is the

1.

hard - est thing. _
hard - est thing. _
must come down. _

2.

3. Well, the

No Woman No Cry

Words and Music by Vincent Ford

First note

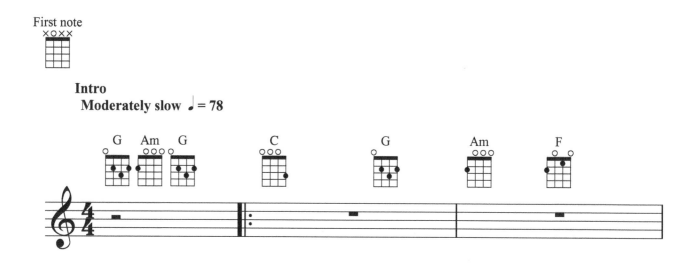

Intro
Moderately slow ♩ = 78

Play 4 times

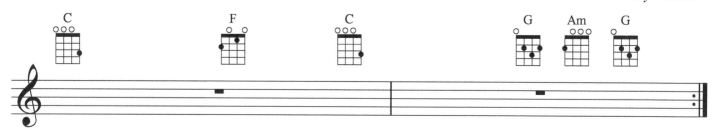

Chorus

No ____ wom - an, no   cry. ____   No   wom - an, no   cry. ____
No ____ wom - an, no   cry. ____   No   wom - an, no   cry. ____

____   No ____ wom - an, ____ no ____ cry.
____   Here, ____ lit - tle dar - lin',   don't shed no tears.

Oh, my lit - tle sis - ter, don't shed no tears. ___

No wom - an, no cry. _____

Guitar Solo

1., 2., 3.

4.

D.S. al Coda

Coda

Chorus

___ through, but while I'm gone... ___

No ___ wom - an, ___ no cry. ___

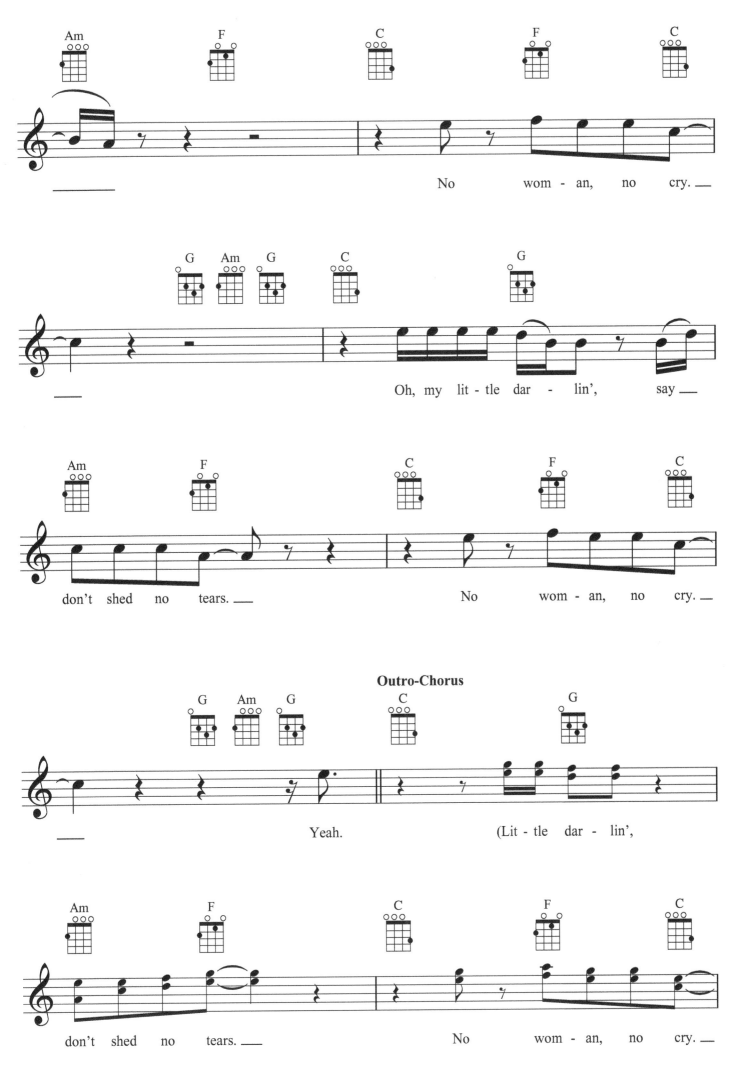

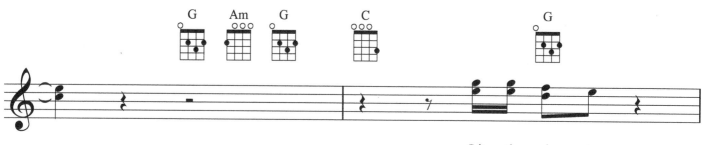

—

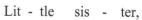

Lit - tle sis - ter,

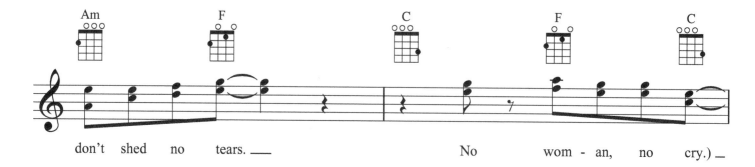

don't shed no tears. ___

No wom - an, no cry.) —

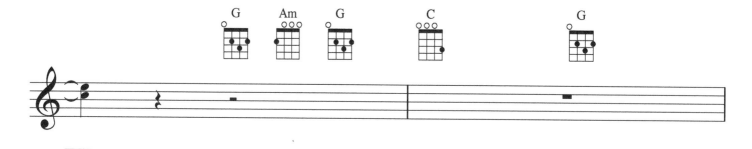

—

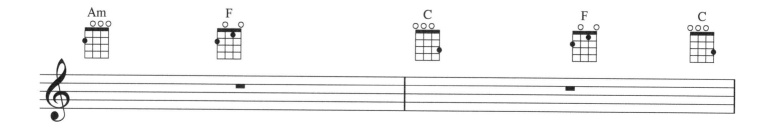

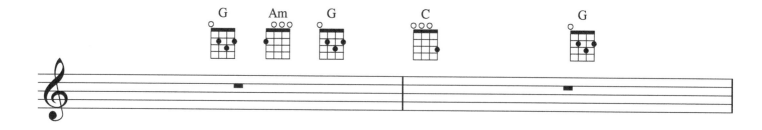

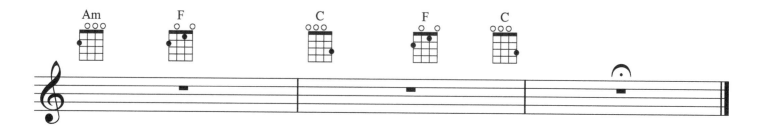

Surfin' U.S.A.

Words and Music by Chuck Berry

3. We'll all be plan - nin' out a

Organ Solo

Guitar Solo

Ev - 'ry - bod - y's gone

Outro-Chorus

surf - in', _____ surf - in' U. S. A. ___

Ev - 'ry - bod - y's gone surf - in', _____

Repeat and fade

____ surf - in' U. S. A. ___ Ev - 'ry - bod - y's gone

Sunshine Superman

Words and Music by Donovan Leitch

1. Sun - shine came soft - ly through my win - dow to - day.
2., 3., 5. *See additional lyrics*
4. *Instrumental*

Could have tripped out eas - y, but I've

changed my ways. ____ It - 'll take time, ____

_____ I know _____ it, but in a while, _____

C

you're gon - na be mine, _____ I know it,

we'll do it in style. _____

Chorus

G   **F**

1., 2. 'Cause I've made my mind up you're go - ing to be mine. _____
3., 5. When you've made your mind up for - ev - er to be mine. _____

1., 2., 4.   **C**

_____ I'll tell you right now, an - y trick in the book, _____

now, ba - by,   that I can find. ____

3., 5.

____ Mm, _____   I'll pick up your hand __

____ and slow - ly   blow your lit - tle mind. ____

'Cause I've made my mind up you're go - ing to be mine, __
When you've made your mind up, for - ev - er to be mine, __

To Coda ⊕

____ I'll tell you right now,   an - y trick in the book, __
____ I'll pick up your hand,

Additional Lyrics

2., 5. Superman and Green Lantern ain't got nothin' on me.
I can make like a turtle and dive for pearls in the sea.
You can just sit there thinkin' on your velvet throne.
I've followed the rainbow, so you can have all your own.

3. Everybody's hustlin' just to have a little scene.
When I said we'd be cool I think that you know what I mean.
We stood on a beach at sunset, do you remember when?
I know a beach where, baby, it never ends.

HAL•LEONARD® UKULELE PLAY-ALONG

AUDIO ACCESS INCLUDED

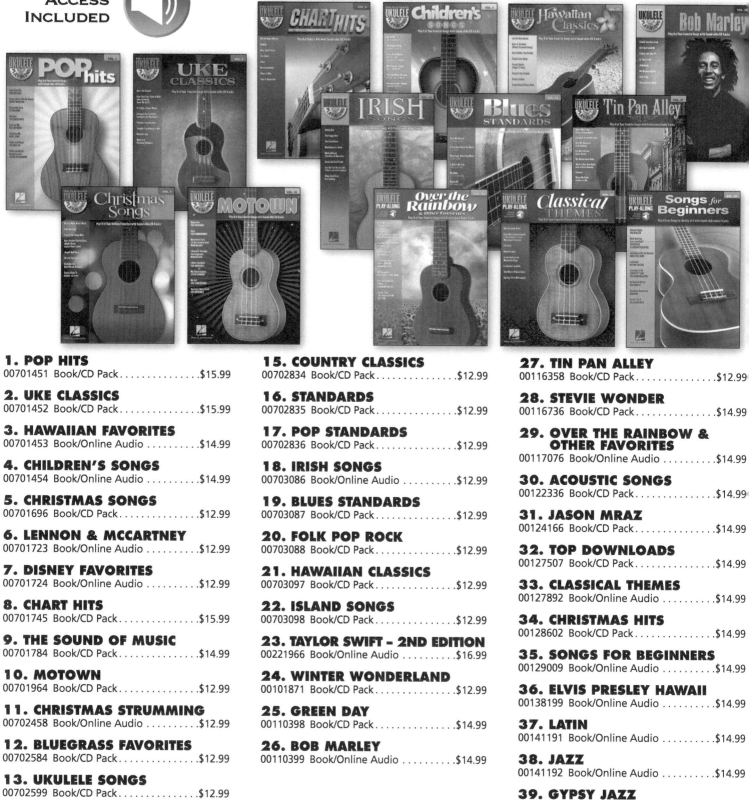

1. POP HITS
00701451 Book/CD Pack...............$15.99

2. UKE CLASSICS
00701452 Book/CD Pack...............$15.99

3. HAWAIIAN FAVORITES
00701453 Book/Online Audio $14.99

4. CHILDREN'S SONGS
00701454 Book/Online Audio $14.99

5. CHRISTMAS SONGS
00701696 Book/CD Pack...............$12.99

6. LENNON & McCARTNEY
00701723 Book/Online Audio $12.99

7. DISNEY FAVORITES
00701724 Book/Online Audio $12.99

8. CHART HITS
00701745 Book/CD Pack...............$15.99

9. THE SOUND OF MUSIC
00701784 Book/CD Pack...............$14.99

10. MOTOWN
00701964 Book/CD Pack...............$12.99

11. CHRISTMAS STRUMMING
00702458 Book/Online Audio $12.99

12. BLUEGRASS FAVORITES
00702584 Book/CD Pack...............$12.99

13. UKULELE SONGS
00702599 Book/CD Pack...............$12.99

14. JOHNNY CASH
00702615 Book/CD Pack...............$15.99

Prices, contents, and availability subject to change without notice.

15. COUNTRY CLASSICS
00702834 Book/CD Pack...............$12.99

16. STANDARDS
00702835 Book/CD Pack...............$12.99

17. POP STANDARDS
00702836 Book/CD Pack...............$12.99

18. IRISH SONGS
00703086 Book/Online Audio $12.99

19. BLUES STANDARDS
00703087 Book/CD Pack...............$12.99

20. FOLK POP ROCK
00703088 Book/CD Pack...............$12.99

21. HAWAIIAN CLASSICS
00703097 Book/CD Pack...............$12.99

22. ISLAND SONGS
00703098 Book/CD Pack...............$12.99

23. TAYLOR SWIFT – 2ND EDITION
00221966 Book/Online Audio $16.99

24. WINTER WONDERLAND
00101871 Book/CD Pack...............$12.99

25. GREEN DAY
00110398 Book/CD Pack...............$14.99

26. BOB MARLEY
00110399 Book/Online Audio $14.99

27. TIN PAN ALLEY
00116358 Book/CD Pack...............$12.99

28. STEVIE WONDER
00116736 Book/CD Pack...............$14.99

29. OVER THE RAINBOW & OTHER FAVORITES
00117076 Book/Online Audio $14.99

30. ACOUSTIC SONGS
00122336 Book/CD Pack...............$14.99

31. JASON MRAZ
00124166 Book/CD Pack...............$14.99

32. TOP DOWNLOADS
00127507 Book/CD Pack...............$14.99

33. CLASSICAL THEMES
00127892 Book/Online Audio $14.99

34. CHRISTMAS HITS
00128602 Book/CD Pack...............$14.99

35. SONGS FOR BEGINNERS
00129009 Book/Online Audio $14.99

36. ELVIS PRESLEY HAWAII
00138199 Book/Online Audio $14.99

37. LATIN
00141191 Book/Online Audio $14.99

38. JAZZ
00141192 Book/Online Audio $14.99

39. GYPSY JAZZ
00146559 Book/Online Audio $14.99

40. TODAY'S HITS
00160845 Book/Online Audio $14.99

HAL•LEONARD®
www.halleonard.com

0719
483

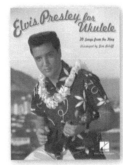

101 TIPS FROM HAL LEONARD

STUFF ALL THE PROS KNOW AND USE

Ready to take your skills to the next level? These books present valuable how-to insight that musicians of all styles and levels can benefit from. The text, photos, music, diagrams and accompanying audio provide a terrific, easy-to-use resource for a variety of topics.

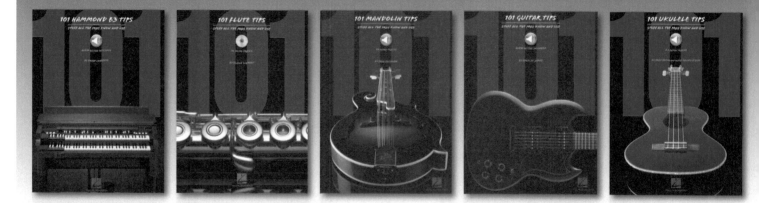

101 HAMMOND B-3 TIPS
by Brian Charette
Topics include: funky scales and modes; unconventional harmonies; creative chord voicings; cool drawbar settings; ear-grabbing special effects; professional gigging advice; practicing effectively; making good use of the pedals; and much more!
00128918 Book/Online Audio $14.99

101 HARMONICA TIPS
by Steve Cohen
Topics include: techniques, position playing, soloing, accompaniment, the blues, equipment, performance, maintenance, and much more!
00821040 Book/Online Audio $16.99

101 CELLO TIPS—2ND EDITION
by Angela Schmidt
Topics include: bowing techniques, non-classical playing, electric cellos, accessories, gig tips, practicing, recording and much more!
00149094 Book/Online Audio $14.99

101 FLUTE TIPS
by Elaine Schmidt
Topics include: selecting the right flute for you, finding the right teacher, warm-up exercises, practicing effectively, taking good care of your flute, gigging advice, staying and playing healthy, and much more.
00119883 Book/CD Pack.................................$14.99

101 SAXOPHONE TIPS
by Eric Morones
Topics include: techniques; maintenance; equipment; practicing; recording; performance; and much more!
00311082 Book/CD Pack.................................$15.99

101 TRUMPET TIPS
by Scott Barnard
Topics include: techniques, articulation, tone production, soloing, exercises, special effects, equipment, performance, maintenance and much more.
00312082 Book/CD Pack.................................$14.99

101 UPRIGHT BASS TIPS
by Andy McKee
Topics include: right- and left-hand technique, improvising and soloing, practicing, proper care of the instrument, ear training, performance, and much more.
00102009 Book/Online Audio $14.99

101 BASS TIPS
by Gary Willis
Topics include: techniques, improvising and soloing, equipment, practicing, ear training, performance, theory, and much more.
00695542 Book/Online Audio $17.99

101 DRUM TIPS—2ND EDITION
Topics include: grooves, practicing, warming up, tuning, gear, performance, and much more!
00151936 Book/Online Audio $14.99

101 FIVE-STRING BANJO TIPS
by Fred Sokolow
Topics include: techniques, ear training, performance, and much more!
00696647 Book/CD Pack.................................$14.99

101 GUITAR TIPS
by Adam St. James
Topics include: scales, music theory, truss rod adjustments, proper recording studio set-ups, and much more. The book also features snippets of advice from some of the most celebrated guitarists and producers in the music business.
00695737 Book/Online Audio $16.99

101 MANDOLIN TIPS
by Fred Sokolow
Topics include: playing tips, practicing tips, accessories, mandolin history and lore, practical music theory, and much more!
00119493 Book/Online Audio $14.99

101 RECORDING TIPS
by Adam St. James
This book contains recording tips, suggestions, and advice learned firsthand from legendary producers, engineers, and artists. These tricks of the trade will improve anyone's home or pro studio recordings.
00311035 Book/CD Pack.................................$14.95

101 UKULELE TIPS
by Fred Sokolow with Ronny Schiff
Topics include: techniques, improvising and soloing, equipment, practicing, ear training, performance, uke history and lore, and much more!
00696596 Book/Online Audio $15.99

101 VIOLIN TIPS
by Angela Schmidt
Topics include: bowing techniques, non-classical playing, electric violins, accessories, gig tips, practicing, recording, and much more!
00842672 Book/CD Pack.................................$14.99

Prices, contents and availability subject to change without notice.

HAL•LEONARD®
www.halleonard.com